THERE WILL BE CHERRIES

ACKNOWLEDGEMENTS

Acknowledgements and thanks to the editors, publications and broadcasts where these poems have appeared: *BBC Talking Poetry, the Buxton Poetry Festival, MacMillan.* Thanks also to the organizers of spoken-word events where so many of us share our work.

"among poets
who neither belong or possess
he planted the poetry of the moment in my ear
I whisper it to you"
– Dinesh Allirajah

"I want to do with you what the spring does with the cherry trees."
– Pablo Neruda

To Jim Sharples and my friends – thank you.

CONTENTS

PLANTING THE CHERRY TREE

The plastic label flapping on its string
promises cherries.
We don't know yet
of the pinching frosts
and endless gales.

For now, our imagination bends
these spindly branches
beneath heavy crops of scarlet.

I wear a white dress laced with sunshine.
Your lips are pursed
to receive the sweet gift.
A blanket is spread on the grass.

Forcing the watering can
into the water-butt, the spout sighs
as icy water rushes in.
We soak and heel-in the tree
beneath wintry allotment clouds.

Soon, one of us will go to the shed
and put the kettle on.
One of us will hold up
a lost and found onion.
One of us will call *tea-up*.

Rubbing your lower back
you lean a moment on the spade,
the robin, at your feet always glad of the digging.
Your muddy face is lovely.
Yes, there will be cherries.

ON THE LINE

On the telegraph pole a herring gull perches
white against black cloud.
Centring the maypole of conversations
it transforms our calls. Hello? Hello?

Words pass up pink legs, behind
its red-ringed eyes and yellow bill,
down every feather's quill and feather-edge
until crackling fractal distances connect

and we shout over our shoulder,
It's a seabird on the phone! A seabird
wants to speak to you. As raindrops
glide to join at each wire's dip

and growth rings in the pinewood
dry and split, we press plastic
to our ears, frowning,
Who is this? Speak up!

EYES OF THE BUS

On the front of the yellow bus
to Howrah Park South are painted
red eyes and black lashes.
The bus sees the brown dog and the man
carrying baskets swinging from a pole.
It sees other busses, it sees you.

The passengers, men in white shirts,
elbows resting in open windows,
turn their heads as the ticket-man beckons,
bellowing over the roar of traffic
Howrah! Howrah!
Howrah Park South!

Your sweating self radiates hesitation:
this bus, that park?
But for a decision you need silence
and here, even spaces between sounds
are filled with sound.

You turn away, knowing that
one damp morning on the 82
between Liverpool and Speke
you'll remember that some buses have eyes,
and you've never been to Howrah Park.

PURE

My body floats. I was bitten by a cobra.
I was…
            whatever you say.

This river holds a darkness
that flashes with colour. Memory unwinds
like lengths of silk.
            I should tuck it in somewhere
but I am too pure for tucking in.

I am a ship of thought, no ropes or sails,
I leave a silver wake
into which you cast handfuls of petals crying
            she was only… she was always… she was…

I remember this bend in the river,
the kingfisher perched here!
If I had a paddle or rudder I could swerve
into the bank, but
there is no more swerving.

Here is where the old jetty rises from the mud.
Black mud – stinking mud
between my toes. I will miss mud.

INCIDENT

Luminous tape
blocks the street,
the wind makes it hum.

A boy puts a finger to the plastic
and tilts his face to his mum,
The wind's talking.

Blue lights strobe our faces
and windows. We text:
shootin in our st

In weeks to come,
kids will do wheelies
past heaps of dying flowers.

He was a good man/bad man.
He stole drugs/a wife/money.
It was a sawn-off/pistol.
He was guilty/they got the wrong bloke.

FLYING?

Bounce
In passing you rip some sequins from her bodice
when you should have been grasping wrists.
Spot-lit and sparkling they fall, hypnotising
the audience. Ooooh…
she bounces in the net. No,
bouncing isn't flying.

Jump
It doesn't last long enough.
It hurts knees.
Fleas are incredibly good at it.

Float
He is passed out on a bench
when the stag party rope him to the helium balloons.
He wakes to the squeak of rubber,
arms and legs outspread in cold air.
He had not known
the river looped round just after the bridge.
He had not known *that* word
was graffitied on the factory roof.

Drugs
The horizon tilts,
the hospital room and everyone in it
peels up and away. Yes, this is flying;
the leather-winged flap of dragons.

Easyjet
You are two minutes late.
The plane had an earlier slot for takeoff.
A young woman with astonishing
false eyelashes points toward the sky.

THE SKI-JUMPER'S HOLIDAY

Palm-trees make me nervous,
Hawaiian shirts flap in slow sea breezes.
Who knows
what makes coconuts decide to drop.

Breath is invisible here.
I stick my head in the mini-bar
to feel the chill on my skin.
Last night my wife found me

alone on the swings,
leaning back and swooping,
the stars captured
between the 'v' of my bare feet.

On the beach
I move sand and watch grains slide.
At night, beneath white sheets
I make mountains with my knees.

THE FIRST LINES OF SONGS

I learned a few songs
> *you do something to me*
from playing records over and over
until Bryan Ferry
> *where have you been, my blue-eyed son?*
sat on my single bed
and told me to get a life.

Apart from that
> *why do birds suddenly appear?*
I only know happy birthday
all the way through
(adding your name if you like).

The rest
> *slow down you move too fast*
is a medley of first lines that can stretch
> *and now, the end is near*
from Birmingham
> *oh little town of bethlehem*
to Liverpool.
> *Penny Lane, there is a barber showing photographs*

Beyond that is nothing but
> *imagine there's no heaven*
hours of la la la and do dooby do.

SPOON

Lovers shaping sleep to find
the closest fit. Singing it to rhyme
with June and moon,
Howling Wolf digs his Spoonful of Blues.
Wood dyed purple from blackberry jam.
Sweetness licked
the way a cow licks a calf.

Not the plastic stirrer of Latte City
but tarnished saints, their arms folded
beneath the heraldic shields
of Sheffield and Kinross.

Puréed apple swoops into focus,
Here comes the aeroplane.
Tap tap the boiled egg, grind
the silver belly into salt.
We kiss the air, blowing it to cool.

LOVE SONG TO A PING PONG BALL

Only you create that perfect sound.
One hundred miles-an-hour
of bat, tabletop and spin.
Only you have the strength of bone
yet are feather-light enough

for bingo-call and kitten-chase.
Ping pong ball I love your skin,
the tiny world of air within.

Released on any ocean shore
you track tides, circling
continents and riding surf
to return and roll to a stop

at my bare feet.
Ping pong ball I love your skin,
the tiny world of air within.

Pale secret, the moon watches
as I flip you high and palm you
whispering into my pocket.
Rubber-bobbled bats are left
facedown on the table, but you

come home with me.
Ping pong ball I love your skin,
the tiny world of air within.

HOLD ON

your PIN number is incorrect
this programme is not compatible
press 1 to continue

come here my darling
hold on

your blood-test results have been mislaid
your call is in a queue
your payment has not been received

come here sweet you
hold on

please verify account details
this mail-box is full
your password is weak

in the night you wake and breathe
precious you, hold on

GALILEO'S LAWS

It never occurred to him to wonder
if weight could affect drop
or if the bridge would distort the splash.

A body, swears the fisherman,
A weighted bag, exclaims the jogger
as ducks arrive in hopeful squadron.

Truth says it was all of those – and none.
And when he drives away
the earth spins beneath his wheels.

Later, uniforms come knocking,
his mam bellowing, Gazza!
Get the fuck down here.

But he's out the bathroom window,
holdall and feet hitting outrigger tiles
at exactly the same time.

He does consider heat rising though,
the helicopter camera capturing
white cartoon lads flowing over black walls.

IMAGINED SEA IN A SOUTH LIVERPOOL TESCO

I open a sliced white and squeeze shell-shapes
from dough. On the silver air-ducts above,
a row of herring gulls watch.
This aisle is dangerously slippery
with yellowish foam and slow-moving starfish.
A seal slaps past so heavily jars rattle
and cornflakes whisper in their boxes.

Beyond the automatic doors, a dog is tethered.
His shabby legs tremble with loss.
The best thing to throw is a half-cucumber
and he gladly slips his leash
to leave paw prints in the sand.
I wish I were brave enough to strip
and gallop gasping into icy water.

As the 82 pulls away I catch a glimpse
of two boys kissing and am glad.
Later I read it was a fight and one
had bitten off the other's ear.
But there is always the sky

and those mysterious things
floating in your eyes. Distant as storm birds
they chase Welsh clouds
and John Lennon's aeroplanes.

THE HARE AND THE CROW

(March, Ribble Valley)

The air sparkles with desire
– he will catch this crow
scratching his field
with her charcoal voice.

Lazily she dances him
across frosted white grass
his dark tracks showing
gaps where he jumps.

His sides heave as she rests
on the kissing-gate
tonguing neatness
into misted tail and wings.

Then, shaking her feathers
into place she descends, fanned
and wide. He leaps
so fur brushes wings.

If they had faces
they'd both be grinning.
If this game had rules
they'd both be cheating.

JUST SO

We open animals like books.
Once upon a time there was a man
and a nub-horned lamb

– both
seeking a grip
on the slick tiled floor.

Here, a calf sucks fingers,
tongue hot and strong, the whites of its eyes
signalling: *The End.*

We live happily ever after.
Look at us pig
through your blond lashes.

Huff and puff,
moo and baa,
make sweet our lamp-lit bedtimes.

QUARRY

siliceous tuff, green-grey and cherty
Who swims in it?
We all do. No one does.
Icy water that makes us thirsty.

Stretton shale, weakly bedded
Dragging school bags we climb, halting
at the sight of black water.
A rusted yellow Citroen see-saws
on its journey to the centre of the earth.

Buxton outcrop with cherty texture
The punctured football sails, we hurl stones,
cheering at each strike.
Gravel hisses with every move.

quartz veining and silification
Which child slipped, hauling at the string
of a drowned kite? All of us remember
the shouting, the echo of tumbling rocks

silico-slate in concretionary layers
as someone's dad slides into the water,
blood slicking his grazed hands as he
shakes the crying child: *never, never, never*

SEEING A FULL MOON

don't we all whisper, *moon, moon,*
our ancestors suddenly
as close as the man next door

who closes his sash window
with such a bang you almost drop the blind,
severing this cosmic show?

In the circle
between finger and thumb
you enclose the shine.

One day you will go naked
into the garden and let moonlight
fall where it may. But for now

you get into bed
needing to feel small.

A FOX VISITS FROM ST JAMES'S PARK

and a policeman nudges another,
icy breath rising in January air.
Adjusting their weapons
they turn to watch and for a moment

Downing Street belongs to weeds
rising up between paving stones
and crows, squatting to graffiti
roof-tiles before taking flight.

Walls creak as invisible armies
of beetles chew at mortar and wood,
while moths, fine as ash, settle
in rugs and ceremonial flags.

The fox slips back into shadow
and the police radio crackles.
All is secure.
Above them, bats dip into the light.

WAXWORKS

We study a row of prime ministers.
Their eyes are well-polished,
finger nails manicured.

This one has freckles.
His mouth looks so real
you could lean in and taste it.

Tourists enunciate each name.
There should be wicks rising
from these slicked heads.

We could gather round and sing.
We could blow at the flames
and make a wish.

COLTRANE

for Dinesh Allirajah 1967-2014

(i) Lazy Bird

She's too many toes for lazy.
Oh come on, stop stretching.
All that lit skin!
The floor offers stockings, a shirt, its arms flung out,
toppled shoes. Time moves like a train;

two espressos and you're old. But now
it's morning, the shower is beating,
soap, steam. Fingers, buttonhole and zips.
Her breath smells of mint,
the hair on the back of her neck is still wet.

As a child she once swung upside down
from the school railings, white socks flashing,
rush-hour traffic roaring in her ears.

Her skirt was a bell of blue, her ponytail
pointing to earth.

(ii) On Green Dolphin Street

We rotate the map and look up,
another sign that doesn't say *Green Dolphin Street*.

People shrug. *Dolphin Street? Green
Dolphin Street?*

The sun catches a window as it opens. We shout up
Dolphin? GREEN Dolphin Street?

We're not lost – only unarrived. We walk in time
to questions: *dolphinstreetgreendolphinstreet?*

Finally a greengrocer leads us out of his shop
and flaps a hand to include

the piled red apples, us, the sky and the sign
above our heads, *Green Dolphin Street.*

(iii) Sun Ship

The sun is drunk
again,
toppling bins,
setting fire to cars.

While dancing,
it trips,
accidentally tearing off
someone's dress.

The sun is arrested,
wrestled to the pavement
beneath a heap
of grunting police.

At the cell door
a solicitor
flips open the spy-hole
only to fall back,

covering an eye
now bloodshot and weeping.
The sun does its work from prison,
filling the sky with stripes.

TEN YEARS TO REMEMBER IT AND FIVE TO WRITE IT

The bumble bee came tapping
at the kitchen window. She heard it
over Jimmy Young and carried out
a teaspoon of honey dissolved in warm water.

The bee, drowsy with cold,
uncoiled its tongue and sucked
this ocean dry.

This moment
is the size of a billboard – a close-up
of black and yellow stripes,
the tea-stained spoon, her knuckles
swollen with arthritis.

When she had two days left,
we melted chips of ice on her cracked lips.
Offering her sweet tea
through a straw, I thought of how
her apron had been bright with flowers.
In that brick back yard she was a meadow.

NINETY YEARS OLD AND YOU TELL THEM

how your fingertips plucked a diamond ring
from the bottom of a pool and how
your damp skin hummed
beneath the lips of a man.
Strangers see your moving lips
and nod, hearing nothing
but your pulse. Never mind

that you rode a Norton 500 and once
walked to Land's End for a bet.
Someone calls you sweetheart
and pats your hand.
No matter, soon enough
you'll throw back the covers

as beyond the hospital car park
a bi-plane is warming up.
Climbing into the cockpit,
buckling the flying helmet under your chin,
you will wave away

the young man in overalls
who stands back to watch
the plane's wheels leave the ground
a little longer at every bump.

DAKINI

When the weight of bone
has been unsheathed,
the Dakini take us.

Released
from tasks of sight and speech
our old self is reflected
in their kind brown eyes.
They flap and tug
as stubborn tendons let go
of the past.

You cannot know
true nakedness until this
moment
when the final syllable of you slips
behind the Dakini's tongue.

Then comes
the winged lift
into glorious nothing.

WESTER ROSS SQUALL

It passes fast, stray clouds
snagged on whitewashed crofts
and blocking empty roads.
A tailwind dips to touch

the loch here and here, so
reflected pines and sky dissolve.
The mountain ridge, screened in fog
is abruptly revealed, its dry rock

silvered with waterfalls.
Crossing the sea, black columns of storm
flicker with lightning as gannets,
white against darkness, arrow and dive.

On the cliff top fence, a blade of sun
makes raindrops tremble with light.
A sheep rhythmically rips at grass,
steam rising from her shorn skin.

WEATHER-COCK

You one-legged fool
with your flat face and squealing spin.
Hammer and saw imagined you,

a black silhouette humming in the gale.
In your shade, a nesting pigeon stirs,
settles warm feathers.

The bolts that root you
rust in the rain,
saplings in the gutters dance.

Voiceless thing,
measuring change.
Who cares now

about east and west?
Who gives a damn
about the wind?

THINKING OF SKIN AND LIFTING ONIONS

I hold the onions high, worms dangling from the roots.
My thumb rubs away mud to reveal
the astonishing gleam – a red
you want to press your lips to.

The sky is emptying – anything will taste good now,
crusts, a coffee bean crunched between teeth.
I see sister hen thrusting her head
under leaves for slugs.

Untangling the worms I drop them back to earth,
blind brothers, stinking of onion. How strange
our words make the world,
on-i-on. Pont-i-ac. Sept-ember.

I think of the mule. The poultice had slipped again.
I held her leg with both hands and tried to pass from my Self
to her Self some power
of heartbeat and muscle.

She shifted as if asking a question.
Tonight I will boil the bandage and hang it with the others,
white streamers swaying on the porch.

When her skin flinches
from a fly or my touch, it moves like water
scrambling from a dive. Last night
she leaned into me
and for a moment we bore each other's weight.

WATER IN YOUR EAR

There is a deep roar of inner space
and for a moment you are on the edge
of something so vast
you grip the sink fearful of tidal shift.

Then it leaks out, the smallest trickle
of warmth on your cheek
and, as soap bubbles pop and fizz,
you hear next door's dog yapping again.

A youth is caught in sunshine
on the bus, the light shines through his ears
– a rosy blush.
The midwife, wiping and wrapping him

whispered something soothing there
but he remembers it only
as a feather's brush on the nape of his neck
whenever he hears an opening fridge door

or the gas fire's hiss before it lights.
We forget each baby comes
fresh from water, ears attuned
to the murmur of ocean. How odd

it must be when air glugs in,
the world sharpening to the dry rasp
of breath, the tiny sounds of parting lips.

WRITING IT ROUGH

(i)

Books are heavy. When a book
is dropped it startles us.
The stone library steps are curved,
readers eroded rock.

(ii)

Rip it up.
Rip it to bits and (if you are lucky)
one scrap will surprise you. The rest
is the litter of what a poem isn't.

(iii)

I find a pen on the train.
The ink only flows if I write in large loops.
I stab and scratch at the paper.
I'd hate to get that letter
the man next to me says.

CLEANSED

My heart was propped open
and all of us could hear the rhythm
of yard-brooms sweeping demons from me.
The bristles hurt. I was mortified.

The demons, still as lizards
(and harmless) were startled into life.
Thrashing, they clutched their heads and cursed.
Buckets of scalding water
swilled and pumices scoured.

I was sore for a long time.
And my heart was not closed properly,
so now the latch makes a clicking noise
when I cough or run.

This scene – this *cleansing*
– was painted onto a plate
and hung on a wall.
I stood at the back of the crowd that gathered.

I didn't need to read the motto glazed in blue
to know it was all a lie.
The halos had been lamps.
God was not present.
I had not been asleep.

NEEDLEWORK

As the last milk-tooth falls
their mouths are sewn
all but for a gap
for morsels of food.

Grandmothers and aunties
armed
with needle and thread
weep but hold firm.

How shocking are the unsewn!
Their split faces, raw
as a wound, teeth
as white as bone.

They bark like dogs.
Such huge wet tongues!

UNDOING

The orange-robed monk
rises from his knees,

shrugging off
a cloak of blue flame.

Planes suck up a bellyful
of bombs.

The rolling news reverses
headlines letter by letter.

Dust and rubble reforms
into houses

and tears roll up faces.
Children and women inhale screams.

TRIP ADVISOR, REVIEWS OF SYNTAGMA SQUARE

Behind the marble tomb of the Unknown Soldier
a stray dog sleeps in the cool shade.
Vikki from New Zealand, poses,
one hand shielding her eyes.
Vikki wears shorts and carries a backpack.
The sky is blue.
Vikki writes: *It's hectic*
here in the heart of Athens.

Pigeons face the same way
in Syntagma Square, each crouched
over its own plump shadow.
The Parliament buildings are pale pink stone.
Warren of Massachusetts writes:
There are benches under lime trees.
Sit back and watch Athens go by.

Changing guards are caught,
pompom feet in mid-stride.
Sandy from Ireland poses
beneath a Cyprus tree.
She wears blue flip-flops and a yellow vest,
The changing of the guard ceremony is fun to watch!
Riot police are nowhere to be seen.

Pensioner, Dimitris Christoulas,
who shot himself in Syntagma square writes:
…I see no other solution than this dignified
end to my life, so I don't find myself fishing through
garbage cans for my sustenance.
Fifteen found these reviews to be useful.

POET, MIGUEL HERNANDEZ

"What does the wind of bitterness want?"

(i)

I am barefoot now, school books hidden in my shirt.
Dry grass stings my shins; the soil is warm.
A flock of serins erupt from thorny scrub.

With two rocks I crack an almond.
A sharp noise,
the sweet milk of nut and spit.
Sheep on the hill pause in their chewing
to look toward me; I wave my stick.

(ii)

People nod hearing the work of my family,
the name of my town: *Miguel Son-of-Shepherd*,
Hernandez-Pobre-of-Orihueva.
I parted the mountains that edge my horizon
and words became mine.
Strangers arrange metal letters,
press ink to pages; Miguel Hernandez.
I stand before crowds who watch my mouth.

(iii)

I remember the heat of her back
through the cotton shirt. My wife's lips
are warm and dry. Our tongues taste of wine.
Night softens fears,
blunts unanswered questions.

Tristes guerras.
Wretched war.
She had always known of this metal prison door,
its weight
severing our future, clean as bitten thread.

(iv)

I enjoy the smell of this pencil,
even the musical sound of it falling
on the floor of my cell.

I draw a tree. Above it
I write poems about the moon.

Franco has me scrub these walls
with my bare hands. His fear
of my words fills me with joy.

(v)

I am a boy herding animals again.
Small sheep and bearded goats,
kids that jump as if the earth
is sending electricity up through all four hooves.
In this dream
they rip at grass with yellow teeth
then arch their tails from hot, sweet scat.
I poke at it with my stick. Yellow flies buzz
into a sky that is everywhere.

DOG IN THE MERSEY

for Anna and Badger Corkill

We scramble down to driftwood and silt
through bulrushes brittle with ice.
Here among tracks of sandpiper and curlew
a plastic hard hat rocks in the wind.
The felt-penned name inside it reads
Joe Benn and beyond it
rests a mud-filled boot.

Ignoring the narrative of J Benn
flailing on rig-ladder or dock-edge,
dog streaks after the real news
of dead rat, fish and mud.
Ears and gums flapping
it's an upwind race.

He vanishes into the frozen reeds,
crashing back in a rainbow of frost.
Sides heaving, he balances
muddy stick with the need to breathe

and raising his chin invites us
to join the chase. He knows
that soon enough doors will close and
he will mark out time
(*bed, get in your bed*) in air heavy with the smell
of women, coffee and forbidden biscuits.

GRATITUDE DIARY

I am happy
again. It's embarrassing. What is it
in sandstone walls that sparkles?
The leaves of the silver birch stir a little
and the pigeon's legs are pink.
When I hold your hand and remember
to chew, life is even better.
Pied wagtails live above us in the gutters,
their song only has one note.
The coffee and complaining was excellent today.

Skips are full of treasure. We can't help but look.
The bagwash is warm and smells of kindness.
My washing line is hung with raindrops.
When we win the lottery we will miss this.

COAL

I held Granddad's hands up to the light,
and he, slack with love, let me
examine smooth nails, his skin
tattooed blue with the dust of coal.

He'd tell me how coal
was crushed forests, how the patterns
of seaweed fronds hide between black seams.
I saw him later, studying the ropes
of veins where I'd traced patterns
and found the initials of his name.

We all coughed in this town.
Grandma coughed so hard
she'd grip the back of a chair
rummaging in apron pockets
for tissues to dab at her eyes.

Granddad's cough was the smallest
– a sharp breath caught in a fist.
My head against the warm shell of his chest
I'd hear the hiss of wash, the scrape
of sea-coal and whistle of wading birds.

FINAL ENTRANCE

Will you tap gently, maybe
fix on a smile and step in *ta-dah!?*
Perhaps you enter
as a child again,
satchel swung and dropped,
peanut butter licked off a knife,
while strawberry crystals dissolve in milk.

Or you could pass, prayer-handed
through the beaded fly-screen of a seaside caravan,
sand gritty on the lino.
Or how about a long unzipping
of tent-flap,
warm orange air inviting you
to fall to your knees and crawl?

I am going to close my eyes – let the scent
of pinched-out shoots lead me
to a greenhouse of tomatoes and red geraniums.
Maybe there is no entrance,
no need to knock, but surely
a pot of freshly made tea, the radio on low.

THE TREE THAT WALKS

The tree that walks sways along the dusty road,
bringing its shadow along the dusty road.
A giant: the tree that walks.

On the forest highway, lorry drivers
hauling neat-cut logs blink and cross themselves,
trying to unsee what they just saw.

It crosses the railway lines, the tree that walks,
so the five-fifteen, all horn and brakes
makes commuters spill their drinks.

On the airport runway, captains
push up captains' hats to scratch their heads.
Jets roar, but the tree that walks does not pause,

its leaves sway and caterpillars swing
from invisible threads. Birds sit tight
on their nests so not one egg falls.

A film truck follows the tree that walks,
footage appears on the rolling news.
A general offers to blow it up. A politician

suggests talks. Headlines shout: TREE WALKS!
Up our dusty road it comes, to a dusty town
where dogs' tongues hang out by miles

and all the grass is dry as bone.
And when the fuss has died down
we fetch pails of water for the tree that walks.

Last night we heard an owl for the first time
and this morning the tree that walks
let its seeds fall like rain.

Today we gather by the derelict barn to watch
the mayor hammer in a new sign:
'Welcome to Walking Tree Town'.

NEWBORN

for Anaia

Thank you, little star,
your rapture at rattled keys
and the curve of a plastic spoon
transports us to a universe
where spacesuits are pink
with crocheted mittens.

Moon-faced we orbit
your gravitational pull
that bends time
with such skill, our skin
wrinkles at your touch.

One day you'll roll your eyes at this
– old people asking:
Where does time go?
You'll inch toward the nearest doorway
smiling politely. Be kind.

If we seem befuddled
it is because, after passing this baby
from lap to lap we looked up
– to see you, tall
and Saturday-night beautiful.

You sent us into a roller-coaster
freefall so wild – be glad
we're only exclaiming
at how you've grown
rather than holding our arms in the air
breathless with shrieking.

TEETHING

Testing resistance of the world
she gnaws the knuckle of your thumb.
The yellow rubber duck shrieks
as her jaws work
to release the idea of teeth.

If she met a king or president
each would retreat,
suits darkened with drool.

Dinosaurs, the fire-engine,
the dog's ear, all feel the heat
of these budding gums.

Serious eyes and firm grip reveal
a force unfettered by the word 'no'.
Cheeks blazing and mouth open,
she topples
toward a world she will eat.

THE TEMPO OF THOUGHT

The wooden seat is hard and reins rest loose
in your hands as the horse leads you home.
In months ahead, the earth
will shove up wheat and weeds
and rain will bog down the fields.

As you sway, the creaking wheels
roll up the day and something slips in
– a memory of how
the flannel sheets marked her thighs
in a language spoken by fingers

and what a fool your brother is
because he should have…

But this thought is broken
as the cart jolts over a rock half buried in mud
and the horse angles to the verge.
The scent of crushed ditch-mint – sharp
 as hands clapped – makes you
sit up straight
and speak your promise out loud.

PHOTOGRAPHING THE WATER SNAKE

She topples, arms grabbing at air.
How quickly

she clambers back out spitting
mud and weed

to stand by her towel at the pond's edge,
hands on hips

and breathing hard (the camera
not yet found).

For a moment
green water had leapt up

and swallowed the day, snakes
tattooed across her rippling skin.

HE LIVED IN A PLACE…

…where there are no clouds. How to describe clouds? I could have said white, could have said grey. Black, I said, they are black and sharp-edged, mostly square. Some are small; others are bigger than buildings. Unimaginable, he said. Do they move? They move slowly, I said, but when they collide they clang and boom like empty oil tankers. Oil tankers? He said. I carried on: if the sky is full of them we have to shout over the noise. Awful, he whispered, how do you stand it? You get used to anything in the end, I said. He put an arm around my shoulders and squeezed, then got up to go. I thought of clouds. Clouds from one horizon to the other in every shade of grey; how they bubbled up to dim the light, swallowing birds and mountains, how they brought the smell of watermelon and snow. How they gave us so much water that everything was divided into things that float and things that sink. Wait! I called as I ran after him; I forgot to tell you about rain.

…where there is no sex. How to explain? A flush rose in my face and I moved my hands vaguely in the air, it's like polishing and being polished – you get shine, but you get sounds as well. He looked blank but politely interested. I tried again. Have you ever eaten something so good it made you close your eyes and moan? He shrugged. I could have gone into the basics; asked to borrow a pen and drawn the curls of tubes and sperm, but he lived in a place where there is no paper. Sex is a kind of dance, I said. It happens once every ten years and millions of people join in. Music comes up through the ground and you can hear it even better lying down. Everyone in the world sings and gets shiny all at once. It must be amazing to see, he said. It is, I said.

…where there is no laughter. It is a kind of possession by spirits, I told him. It happens when you least expect it. It's best to sit down before you fall over. Your mouth won't close and you can only exhale. The spirits come streaming out shaped like birds and barking dogs. Can they be shaped like clouds? he said. No, these spirits are all colours; they move fast and use laughing as a chance to jump from one body into another. I can't explain really. I wish I could, but I can't. He looked at me for a long time, until I turned away. Your face is raining, he said.

"HANG ON A MINUTE, LADS. I'VE GOT A GREAT IDEA"

It's all much the same:
old farts complaining about boom and bust and pissed
at how close they came to a decent pension.

But like the Italian Job we've ended up
with the whole shebang seesawing on a cliff's edge
– a fall made inevitable by slide of bullion.

But what do we know; us old ones who forget
to take gloves off to text, and remember
when telephones had real bells.

Completing the date-of-birth-box we scroll down,
and down some more, the mouse-wheel clicking past
the other recessions, riots, Thatcher.

Here's your first job, first colour tv and Granddad
spilling his tea with the laughing,
You're only supposed to blow the bloody doors off.

SKINBOUND

today your body is no longer confined
in a downward slope of spine to the ends of toes and fingertips

today is not about small sips of the world
taken through tired eyes and skin

today you open and colour comes
from you and to you, and through and through

whispering the jazz rhythm of brushes on skin
dancing like light through single malt

and your particles forget
the worries they have about being arms and legs

your ten knuckles and the busy ventricles of your heart
and your nuclei abandon tasks of multiplication and division

and the atoms of your lips and nipples say fuck it
let's dance

and the colours spread and the gap between
you and everything else opens and closes like gills

transforming dark into tie-dye silk
the weft and warp unwinding you

into someone else, something else, everywhere else
today you escaped the endless chatter of you

for a moment you opened like blossom
for a moment you fell like blossom

AID

It is a line that begins
with the smallest of tremors,
dust hissing from cracks in the ceiling
and the harmonic of crockery.

You are the reason for this queue,
your cotton swabs, your calm eyes over the mask.
And hours later they still come.
Strangers shouldering up strangers,
shirts and tea-towels pressed to wounds
and everyone coughing.

An old woman is brought to you
in a squeaking wheel-barrow, her husband
repeating the same question
as his hands weigh the terrible air.

And here is a man carried on a torn-off door,
your knees crack as you crouch.
His eyes meet yours, then close,
accepting your need for privacy
while you assess what he has become.

CURSES

When our country ran out of swearwords
we were allocated a handful at birth,
five of this, six of that,
I cannot tell you which (I'm saving mine).

Once, curses were everywhere
– lost things, dropped things!
I've only used one so far, I was eight
and a boy tore a button from my coat.

The sensible save theirs
for childbirth and disaster,
others sell them to eager crowds
who cover their mouths and dance with glee.

No one can stop us imagining them though…
the rhythms of a shaken paint can,
a blank white wall,
your finger on the hissing nozzle.

PRACTISING EMPTINESS AT CALAIS

"... the world would rather we didn't exist," – Karim Durrani

In dreams that stink of diesel
tailgates tumble open, loved ones inside
beckoning,
come, come.
Through shanty-towns of canvas and plastic
the lorries queue. Cargo of the world
behind taut straps and bolted doors.

This grey strip of sea is so narrow
one scar-faced boy shrugs
off his leather jacket
saying that he would rather walk.

On flattened cardboard boxes
the schematics of airbrakes and exhausts
are mapped. Spaces are measured,
air-holes marked.
Emptiness must be mastered
so detection-dogs will pass,
tails wagging
– carbon monoxide detectors will read *all* c*lear.*

Those who name villages and cousins,
those who talk in their sleep
of soldiers and bombs,
make the pine-tree air-fresheners swing.
In the stillness of motorway car parks
they make St Christopher catch the light.

HUNTING SEASON

We ran away that weekend
– but we ran away most weekends,
 packing a bag with biscuits, a box of matches
 and stubs from her step-dad's ashtray.

 It was hunting season
 and as we crawled the miles of farm ditches,
 hunters shot at sky.
When the pheasant thudded at our feet
 its lolling head and wings were shockingly warm.

The golden retriever wagged
 its whole back end
 when it found the two nine year old girls crying.
 It sat obediently to watch us dig.
We came home in the dark, stinking
 of smoke and sick from eating raw cabbage.

 Her dad or mine
 hefted a belt across his open palm.
 At dawn, pebbles would crack at my window
 and I'd dress and run away once more.

A few years later, one of us – I don't remember
 which – ran off with a boy on a motorbike
 and we never saw each other again.
 But I do recall how carefully
 that bird was wrapped in the green school jumper
 and how our grubby hands smoothed
 the glossy orange feathers.

THE BEST THING ABOUT CONFERENCES

It's nearly coffee break.
Here in seminar room four,
someone wheels in a trolley
of clinking cups and a plate of donuts.

We are team-building
and have made rocket ships
out of each other. The presenter is careful
not to raise his voice or fold his arms.

His eyes are closed.
We nudge each other
nodding at the trolley.
On the whiteboard

he has spelled
D R E A M. We are visualising
our goals. Shut your eyes, he says again.
Someone's stomach rumbles.

The trolley is brushed metal,
the stacked cups are white, the plates
are white, the donuts are pink
and brown with sprinkles.

SKY FORGIVE US

We rarely look – at most
a quick glance to check for rain
or double-take at a fat moon.

Tongue-tip poking, children crayon
cartoon suns over rainbow arcs:
Richard Of York Gives Battle.

It's self-preservation, otherwise
we'd be stumbling into traffic,
gawping at the milk-edge of galaxies

and the mackerel silver
astonishing three counties.
Cathedral of sky forgive us

our desks and clocks. We should run outside
to join the crowds – *what did I miss?*
Everyone sighs, *Pink, so pink.*

The last slice of sun
drops behind a hill
– there's a smattering of applause.

Forgive us sky, our furry heads
and crooked partings,
our shoved-up umbrellas, hats and hoods.

Forgive us our clumsy words
for cloud, the brutal
bookends of *dawn* and *dusk.*

Understand the hand
that shields when we face you.
Forgive us our rooftops.

RE RE RE

Dive to where the router's surging green
splits into another spectrum.
No jet-skis, beach balls

or rubber-duck race,
each one labelled
with someone's name.

Nothing can follow you here
without aeons of evolution
and the whistles and clicks

are shadowy things living
in faith of the open mouth
and lips of phosphorous bait.

THERE WILL BE CHERRIES

MANDY COE

Printed by imprintdigital
Upton Pyne, Exeter
www.imprintdigital.net

Typesetting and cover design by narrator .
www.narrator.me.uk
info@narrator.me.uk
033 022 300 39

Published by Shoestring Press
19 Devonshire Avenue, Beeston, Nottingham, NG9 1BS
(0115) 925 1827
www.shoestringpress.co.uk

First published 2016
© Copyright: Mandy Coe

The moral right of the author has been asserted.

ISBN 978-1-910323-54-0

FOR POETRY MAKES NOTHING HAPPEN

"a way of happening, a mouth." – W. H. Auden

When the olive trees stand unbroken
and black smoke has not risen
from a village that has not yet fallen,
let nothing happen but sunlight
playing its tricks between leaves,

and let this old man at the table
who does not weep or run and hide,
only wipe his mouth with his sleeve
after a meal of sweet wine and ripe tomatoes.

When oiled bullets lie boxed in rows
and maps rest, the borders not
arrowed in red, let nothing happen except
leaves being brushed from the table
and talk about worn tyres and fat avocados.

A round pebble is placed on the cloth
to roll in an unsteady path toward a girl
who glances at the boy. Let nothing happen.

BUD

We are planted upside-down,
legs waving as they root into sky.

Our voices are muffled, no one listening
but the worms. In this new night

the worms are kind and soft,
slicking past lips and our closed eyes.

The earth is a head, a brain. The earth
is a halo for planted angels.

I love this way of life.
Light was overrated, the decisions – exhausting.

Let's bud; ten toes,
ten leaves, dancing and green.